ABOUT THE AUTHOR

Jim Hale is a retired senior high school teacher, who specialised in English literature. He taught for 40 years, in country NSW and city schools. He has three children and eight grandchildren, who have added to his wide experience of the joys and tribulations of life. These experiences are expressed in his poetry, written at first for family and friends, and now shared more widely in published form.

JIM HALE

Facing East at Sunset

AUSTIN MACAULEY PUBLISHERS™
LONDON • CAMBRIDGE • NEW YORK • SHARJAH

Copyright © Jim Hale 2023

The right of Jim Hale to be identified as author of this work has been asserted in accordance with section 77 and 78 of the Copyright, Designs and Patents Act 1988.

All rights reserved. No part of this publication may be reproduced, stored in a retrieval system, or transmitted in any form or by any means, electronic, mechanical, photocopying, recording, or otherwise, without the prior permission of the publishers.

Any person who commits any unauthorized act in relation to this publication may be liable to criminal prosecution and civil claims for damages.

A CIP catalogue record for this title is available from the British Library.

ISBN 9781398400726 (Paperback)
ISBN 9781398400733 (ePub-e-book)

www.austinmacauley.com

First published 2023
Austin Macauley Publishers Ltd®
1 Canada Square
Canary Wharf
London
E14 5AA

DEDICATION

To my sons Ashley and Kerry who always encourage me and to my daughter Alana who always laughs with me.

ACKNOWLEDGEMENTS

My son Kerry Hale for inspiring a cover design. My partner Beth for computer assistance with submission of these poems.

POEMS

1. Facing East at Sunset 9
2. Snake Road 10
3. First Frost 11
4. The Ball 12
5. Old Houses 13
6. Still Feel 14
7. Sandhill Sonnet 15
8. Woodstock (The Old Home in Burwood and Its Parking Lot) 16
9. Off-day 17
10. Elegy for the Mad 19
11. The Silent Sea 21
12. Too Much Time to Think 22
13. The Old Punter 24
14. Tavern Reverie 25
15. Modern Madness 26
16. Colonial Gardens 27
17. Old Church 29
18. The Knees 31
19. Prawn and Barbie Night with Old Mates 32
20. Herbalists 34
21. Feral She-Cat 35
22. Headline 36
23. Coming Up the Fourth at Marrickville 37
24. Stairwell Graffiti 38
25. Working Through Hoyle 40
26. End of a Marriage 43
27. Chasing Roos at Coona 45
28. Southern Highlands Train 46
29. A River 48
30. The Imperial 50

31. A Cell 52
32. Milkman and The Maggies 53
33. A Little Spanish 55
34. Annibal the Dental Mechanic 58
35. Anzac Day Speakers 60
36. Formal 62
37. Michael's Garlic Crop 63
38. The Ruined Lighthouse at Cape St George 65
39. Overtaken 66

1. Facing East at Sunset

You say – I'll leave when it gets to the trees,
but the shadow moves relentlessly and
when it's reached that point
you say – no the ridge above that,
when it hits that I'll go ...
but it hits the ridge and suddenly
the air is totally totally still,
and the light is going
and the dark begins to come down
as the dark always will.

2. Snake Road

The amazing anaconda
writhes in and out along the way
sections constricting, sections stretching longer
stealthily muttering
full of menace –

inside the umbilical beast
voices mutter mutter away
no jollity as in a conga
stuttering in quiet desperation
from insufficient pay to pay –

what bulk there is what power
that holds so many of us in dread –
who would not face the anaconda
except for the ribs that bind us there
and what we cannot see instead?

3. First Frost

First frost of the year has nestled like dandruff
on lower street lawns still in shade,
the first pinch of winter snickers tips of things
and arrival of the shortest day
is easily measured now –
"two months in and two months out"
is race memory of older folk,
whose men all minded these parts
in May and autumn
where first frosts were noted harbingers
of valley-smoked winters to be borne,
before the coming of the new springs.

The serious frosts of winter
tie down the place like "the arthritic gout":
the withering sinews of summer's runs
are screwed by the marbling of uric acid,
and healthy things
are chapped and splintered.

But, as with the unwinding that comes,
the marbled immobility will break down
and with it the promise that will always play out –
the valley will begin to ooze the early spring,
and the first frost of yesterday
will be gone.

4. The Ball

A curling ball
holds its line defying law
and loops towards the crouching man
bat raised in indecision –
it hits the pitch
it grips and rips
past the searching blade –
I turn again lope in and hook the ball
into resistant air
and it spits again with a will to deceive ...

I am the deceiver
my wrist the line
that hooks the bait
not once but always
always all ways
deceiving mine
and the batsman's fate ...

I see the curve as I look at a wall
I hear the fizzing in my sleep
the image exists and thrives
from incomprehensible deep –
I have bowled this ball a million times
Its shape and sound a symbol of soul –
a million times?
I have never bowled this ball at all.

5. Old Houses

If there are such things as spirits,
I hope they inhabit old houses.
What a waste if not.

Once they would have entered for the first time,
in pride and hope,
the dirt floor swept,
the bed covered in a mother's old crochet;
elsewhere implements, pots and everything
that expectation brings.

And from that bed a child,
and beside it a cot,
later a partition,
later still an extra room.
Not so later still,
two small graves,
some distance removed from the vegetable patch,
and flowers,
from the garden to the window sill.

What a waste if the ache of love
did not inhabit old houses still.

To see them now, small,
sadly gaped in roof and wall,
beside a football field, an agricultural school,
stirs something in heart and head.
I hope the spirits are still there,
making love on a crochet-covered bed.

6. Still Feel

I can still feel

the curving curling lines of your back
and see your eyes two inches from mine,
closed but intense
and thin beads of water
on your cheeks ...

I can still feel

your fingers on mine,
the exquisite points touching
like tongues
each to each ...

I can still feel

the sense of height
the unreal headiness of space
the minutes and hours through the night
that raced then stopped
and the light at the end,
soft and serenely grey.

I can still feel

because of you.

7. Sandhill Sonnet

Framed against a sky as wide as earth and blue as space,
Ringed by the first green and a hymn of birdsong and surf,
The sandhill in the morning is a living holy place,
A pastel crib of eon's age, the shifting bed of our first birth,
Cool sheet-and-pillow sand, a hallowed place,
A world of rolling swelling ebb and flow
Where godless crabs and gulls attend with dignity and grace
Such birth as cannot help but grow.

I watch your head against the newness, cradled in blue,
Feel your surf-pulse rhythm rocking over me –
We love and laugh and all our loving and laughing are new
Ad we know that all there is to see, we can see –
And as we leave, singing in each other's flesh,
We leave the hill to others, new, clean, fresh.

8. Woodstock
(The Old Home in Burwood and Its Parking Lot)

Not for us the tameness
of lame loving
on the edge of sleep,
nor for us
the gentle subsiding
at the end of the day
nor a somnolent drift
at the end of the week.
Not for us.

Not for us to cringe
at the coming of the cold
or the end of heat,
not for us
the withdrawal surrender
or retreat
at summer's end.
Not for us.

For us
the brashness the outrageous
leap of trust,
the wild satiating
overflowing
liberating
sheer
woodstock-autumn-clear

abandon to lust –
for us.

9. Off-day

The image of a naked man at the edge of the surf,
bent low, head close to sand
prompts the early tourist, disgusted
to quickly veer –
the man convulses and disgorges
what looks like sea water and
unrecognizable pink stuff
and head flops down, arse to the sky.

A man sits at breakfast munching toast and jam
waiting for the phone to ring –
clothed neatly in ironed shorts
and pocketed short-sleeved shirt,
he has expectations today of work –
it's well enough into term for "mental health days to kick in
or the odd bit of long service leave –
but the phone remains quiet
and by nine it's clear the day is gone.
So something must be done
rather than sit there and grieve
and so a plan: drink.
The Lennox pub fronts the beach,
so close to the surf,
the windows are regularly cleaned of salt;
right now the doors are closed.

Seated, knees splayed in front,
the man stares at the water,
the breathing waves, the sea beyond –
opening time is too far away;
shoes come off, socks, shirt, shorts, undies
and standing
he walks deliberately into the water,
accepting unflinching as it moves
up his legs, pelvis, waist
till confronted by a larger swell
he dives under and emerges

clumsily swimming ...
strange to the casual watcher
watching the now small figure bobble out
beyond the surf,
strange that no exhilarating display
of any kind could be observed –
and then the figure is gone.

Gradually aware of the sun
on his bum and back
and noise from inside the pub,
the figure splashes face and head,
gingerly retrieves his clothes –
redressed, the shirt clings but will soon dry
and hair pushed back,
and inside to stares,
he buys a schooner and
the raw throat responds to a few gulps
while one thought repeats:
it was a long swim back.

10. Elegy for the Mad

(For people I met on the Bay run ...)

Some used to inhabit hutches at Rozelle
down near the bay run facing the water:
the waters change – sequined, dressed up,
alive in one mood, asbestos-grey in another,
in motion light, slab-hard when still.

I envied the eyes of the mad I met
with their vestiges of sanity opalised in rock.
So what of shambles, incoherence, patronage and shit,
the sadness of of others still on the spit
if eventually they were well and truly beyond
the shock of tendon-tearing madness and dread?
No sorrow for them –
pity the sane instead.

I have gone mad,
not uncommon I think and
can still feel it not far away –
this is why I write
to ward off stay upright
or else willing
let leaden head crash
down on table
beaten
still-eyed unshaven sluttish reeking
nose veined red ...

her form
is shimmering in the heat
I bluster stutter
incoherence swelling
last out
split face
pink
splatting on windows

not again
again
I am apart
I am with the mad
this is my elegy
I think I see water from me bed.

Now I write a poem every day.

I think I see water from my bed,
Dressed up, working with the setting autumn sun,
Alive in moving light of meandering russet red,
Mirroring the ambers whose liquid palettes run
And spill all over and ripple through my mind.

11. The Silent Sea

Are we the first who ever burst
into that silent sea?
Coleridge and Carl Sagan
posed that question:
what if there is no-one else but us?
Are we to populate time and space,

to energize other life forms
with supernatural ease,
behind the pyramids of planet X?
Life forms built of synthetics
not tissue – us –
will people the UFOs
that look at our present handiwork
with pride –
by then we would not blush.
Will we serve as gods
to multiple millions
in multiple million years time?
(We will laugh at their simplicity,
having tagged us with infallibility
benevolence,
and infinity of grace
all-loving capable of sacrifice ...)

Are we that race?

12. Too Much Time to Think

Quite frankly,
it seems to me that Hamlet was doing
a student prince thing at university,
a Danish Lanza lapping up country matters,
lying between maid's legs,
buying for the inn and
draining draughts of Rhenish,
chorusing loud into the nights,
and later honey-dewed vows flowing from his tongue,
when necessary "a scholar's eye",
always a glass of fashion and the mould of form.

How could he miss,
how could he not love it?

Why oh why did the old man die?

Can you imagine?
Rushed preparations, rushed explaining,
promises of "soon, not forever",
love-making urgent and long and leave-taking
in a pre-dawn light,
because he had been sent for
and could not say no.

And they were waiting.

Back in Elsinore,
the funeral,
the dirge-paced time,
the courtly mourning black,
the politics,
the cold,
the waiting,
the lack of mirth,
of exercise,
(except for the girl

to while away the time with,
trinkets, love tokens and tales of the world –
love her? of course –
she was worth the effort despite her father) ...
but mostly the waiting,
and then the wedding,
ah yes the wedding,
and then more waiting and
Ophelia's brother heading back to Paris –
then that damned ghost!

Who wouldn't go mad?

And who would have thought of all this stuff,
of this variation of a prince on the brink,
except that he spends half his life on the road
with just too much bloody time to think?

13. The Old Punter

At the pub on the corner
of Marrickville Road,
a man comes in,
well, agonises in,
grimacing as he puts his weight
on the instrument,
the four poster walking stick,
his means for a drink and a punt;
his hair's brushed back,
slicked but grey,
maybe a dashing Harry Lime
some time not long past,
but now his lips are puckered
from wrinkles.

He gasps for breath
after each gulp of his schooner.

Around him,
the punters check the form
and the race caller gets orgasmic
at Murwillumbah.
He wobbles and chats,
drinks, gulps, gasps
and steadies –

and as I watch,
he manages at TAB ticket
and winks brashly
at the girl who serves him.

14. Tavern Reverie

A girl polishes a brass rail
at ankle level,
her bottom a foot from the floor,
packed buttocks squeezing into
her dress shortened by the stretching;
so the old witless drive
stirs itself,
stretching in its pocket.

Oblivion stares at us,
pock-marked
no-nosed
oblivion,
a million star-times of
nothingness,
a sink-black void into which
all things could fall and
not fill –
and here is the brassy tavern,
I think of sex.

15. Modern Madness

Madness: the opiate then, the opiate today,
Escape to the mariner's ancient time,
escape through outrageous law's delay,
poets robbed of word and rhyme
with those that weren't sent for dead.

All were sent for who rose at dawn
and picked up the sickle and sword
for the new messiah: bowed since born,
they scythed or were scythed and turning inward,
did what they did out of dread.

And the hermit, the herbalist, living alone,
found remedy, grace in seclusion
But were cracked or burnt or blasted with stone
by the pious who worshipped confusion,
and the marrow of sanity bled.

16. Colonial Gardens

The gardens of a younger Australia
were not encroached on by
glint-edged suburbs, festooned
with the panoply of ever-bulging nurseries –
back then could still be discerned
the doily/lace/crochet of
heirloom plants lovingly brought from
the old country and nurtured,
as a heritage,
a continuity of sorts, a link.

Colonial gardeners constructed
their new-world inner-world
flanked by the tall and ancient gums and ash,
dwarfed often by these primeval forests,
establishing footholds of European self-sufficiency
in a hostile non-white land,
and having done, looked out from
the security of gardens
filled with familiar plants ...

And gradually appeared
flowered archways,
gravel and mellow brick paths,
lantanas and hydrangeas,
brick and quartz stone edgings
and complex geometries of beds of
shrub and veg,
compiled with faith and optimism
from bricks, bottles, timber, terracotta,
shells and bones
and all variety of stone.

Staring boldly in pose from acid-aged photographs are
standing men and seated women,
whose hopes were symbolised in
gardens such as these,

who on arrival heard no familiar voice,
no touch, no odour,
not even a familiar toy
of previous lives,
but whose labour
remade their world,
and furnished food for their young,
and ancient roses for
long lost burial grounds.

17. Old Church

A small stone church
still stands by the side of the road,
winding into Queanbeyan –

sandstone
with half one wall gone,
solid but fragile,
it stands alone
and testifies to –

small congregations
in a smaller time,
men with white foreheads
like lace doilies
over wooded faces –

ankle length dressed women,
descending lines of children
in ironed bibs
and Sunday braces –

plaintive songs of praise
offered up in thanks,
but underpinned by
desperate need for rain –

shiny-faced weddings,
graced by walls
stacked with glads and violets
so that the walls themselves
are impregnated –

dour funerals of course,
with as many parents
keening their young
as the young farewell them –

and outside waiting
tethered horses, drays,
the lonely bush,
crowded with life.

18. The Knees

Did they always show signs of wear –
ligament damage (unheard of then),
come good then go bad again
and finally beyond repair,
necessitate
a crutch
or a stick?

Christ's knees, being young of course,
would have held him up quite well,
but broken, his diaphragm blasted to hell,
that was the crunch,
the dead and the quick.

Rather be the ghenghis, Khan,
knees strong enough to root with or wrestle –
died with a ruptured penis vessel.
Untrue? But what a bloody good yarn –
If I had to go
that'd be my pick.

One day, briefly, I'll look down on me,
last breath gone, on my back, or on grass,
and not enough time to reflect on the past,
I'll probably simply laugh at the knees –
just as the light goes out
at the wick.

19. Prawn and Barbie Night with Old Mates

Why? It's difficult to say
don't really know why I went
there was conscription but heh
I wasn't at uni, wasn't queer or bent,
like you bastards – I just did my time –

my old man – poor old bastard – he was in the war
"Bloody long-hair poofters afraid to fight"
but it wasn't that so much – I wanted more than
an apprenticeship and plumbing day and bloody night
and I was young and fit and not like now
in my bloody prime –

and all those stories they wrote, hardly any of em true
those fuckin sly VC and old lady or young kid
you shitbags protesting back home yeh all of you
what did youse know about stayin alive
or what we did?
We fought for Australia and could've won.
Where's the bloody crime?

Well yeh we smoked and got pissed but innocent stuff like that –
we only killed because we had to –
they'd have fucking-well killed us.
they blew old Al's balls off – a land mine near Nui Dat –
I spewed after seeing it – Christ was a noise what a fuss
I think I think that we sort of ... well you had to be there
at the time ...

we went – after that – a bit made a bit feral
and there was this village with these skinny women no men
and there was a lot of shit an angry thing goin on
and we were really down and then
what happened wasn't anyone's fault wasn't mine
it didn't reach the papers right at the time
and most of it's bullshit
she was more like twenty than bloody nine.

Yeh Helen knows about it
but I didn't tell her for a long time
till after the boys were born ...

it's difficult to know why ...
still it was a rotten bloody time

I still hate that rotten fucking tune "I was only 19" ...
yeh they should be home from the hospital soon.

20. Herbalists

Women begged for potions
when their children sneezed and fell down
or husbands wasted hollow-eyed –

Farmers pleaded and ranted
for means of revenge
when crops failed or animals died –

people dealed for whatever
postponed their fate
of the stake-thin lives they lived,
and barely comprehended
why a herb did this
or a root did that
or a flower or a mould
or a fermentation –

but when times went bad
or a purge was due
or some heresy had become too bold
we called herbalists witches
and burned them
till they slithered down,
their body fat
staining the earth
like molten human candle wax.

21. Feral She-Cat

Paws padding noiselessly,
tail a periscopal tester of the wind,
body flattened, a parody of freestyle dance,
her eyes see through dark walls:
from the gorge she materialises,
sliding across moonlit gaps
with the assurance of a million years.

Feral she-cat,
your eyes see through domesticated beings
and in yours can be seen my origins,
past and perhaps my future –
what reign of disembodied hell
may blast me back to gorges,
deep within safe darkness,
from which I have to pad
for sanity and food?

Your eyes turn
and lock on mine –
my ears go flat,
I am stealth,
I will survive.

22. Headline

Was it a morning like this when the bomb went off?
Did the early morning sun glint off the water
and powder-blue skies glisten down?
Did the white-hot instant singe and scale and
the skin peel like paint,
the sky/water blanch, the blue fading,
the horizon bend and the air push inward
in a single crack and stretch of time?

I see a headline "Hanged!"
and another image –
trouser legs swaying soundlessly
in a slow white wind.

We are all addicts.

23. Coming Up the Fourth at Marrickville

At the bottom they pause
and survey the hill,
then wade into it
like convicts on an early morning mountain climb –
they drag their buggies
and tools of trade,
as strongly forged as leg irons and chains;
they do not survey the vista
that builds behind them,
they are single-minded
and in their dreams they dream of birdies
and women and ale –
and as they lean,
the pressure builds
like good head
frothing to the top
and levelling off,
subsiding
with a sigh
then dropping down in gulping breaths.

24. Stairwell Graffiti

I remember that on the rediscovered walls of Pompeii
some pimp had written
"Doris will give a good time for twopence" –
or maybe it was Doris.

Today the signers and artists work billboards and
overpasses,
obvious toilet doors and walls
and building surfaces, anything at all
that will take some ink or paint –
and of course shirts/blouses on last days of school.

Now as then the graffiti goes on,
in fun or frustration, need or hate,
in some will to create
or just be seen – but few survive
the dwindling memory glands that suckle history.

I imagine the write poised
with chisel, charcoal, can or pen,
the message skipping through the nerve ends of the brain,
the shapes the letters framing
under the hand that serves the need
and the process is done.

The process is done,
the judgement of it
beyond the writer's range –
what old Khayyam knew was right:
the writ not the writer is the essence of it
though piety or other's wit and time
cancel most lines again and again.

And if the only have stairwells
on which to record what they have to say
and they've been cleaned many times,
new-bare walls are hard to resist –
I watch a boy scrawl
what he wants us to know –
TEACHERS SUX.

25. Working Through Hoyle

You have to follow the set rules
when you learn by working through Hoyle –

Canasta samba
red dog (with matches)
pinochle hearts (rickety kate)
cribbage solo
jackpot poker
(never draw to an inside straight!)

Gulargambone,
flat drawn out nasal vowels:
three twenty-year-olds
for lack of something better to do,
meet each Wednesday night
at the home of a local postal worker
and his wife,
and decide to work through Hoyle.
It passes time.

Canasta is tricky, a lot of cards to hold
but is mastered by the end of term one.
In supper breaks – meringue tarts, lamingtons –
Shirley comes up:
bright, sporty, pretty, dark,
she should have gone to senior school
but her shearer-father has eight kids
so a spot is found on the hospital staff –
a nurses aid.

Hearts is deceptively simple –
in later years, dodging rickety kate
is quite a successful computer trick
but now,
the thrill of dodging the scoring cards
is matched by
capturing the whole bloody lot and

forcing the others to take
the maximum score.
Over tea and chocolate monties
the incident at the pub,
the furore of Friday night is discussed:
John the copper dragged the boy down
the total length of the spiral stairs,
head clanging on each metal step,
dumped on the concrete floor in his own blood.
Somehow alive,
he complains next day in the bar
of the world's worst headache,
hangover he thinks ...
(he will be dead
before the year drifts away –
drowned in the billabong
in a foot of water,
scared witless by the "black mass"
the knowing ones say ...).

Pinochle is started
but dumped for cribbage –
two had played it young
learning like bingo callers
the fun of rhyming slang.
Before supper,
half a brick lands on the roof
and a wild screech of tires:
it's become personal –
the freedom riders on the freedom bus
are travelling through N.S.W.
and hatred
for whatever reason
is levelled at us.

The postal worker's wife explains
and we say we understand –
she comes from here
and has to live in the town.
We play three-handed five hundred
with a dummy hand

and a similar bash at solo
with modified rules,
but it isn't the same
one player down.
Supper becomes chips and beer:
the brawl at the bowling club comes up –
who through the first punch?
and what about that kick in the gutter?
The eye was closed for almost two days
and it was difficult to hear
what the police said.

Contract bridge:
call, overcall, double, redouble,
above and below the line,
numbers of odd tricks –
we flicked the whole lot
and played drunken games
of "bullshit" until the year was dead.

According to Hoyle?
Even after all these years
the rules remain somewhere in the head.

Canasta samba
red dog (with matches)
pinochle hearts (rickety kate)
cribbage solo
jackpot poker
(never draw to an inside straight!) ...

26. End of a Marriage

I am only partly consumed by fire.

The season's mood
is in the air like Neapolitan cooking,
in a Haberfield backyard
Sunday morning.

There is warmth in the sky,
elemental sensuous,
autumnal only on brisker nights,
precursors of antipodean winter which is
cold but snowless and
lacks the depth of contrast of northern winters,
lacking the fire and the ice.
In the flight path
the planes wing in from the north
from ice and fire.

Change is not so definite here
a sense of history does not dominate –
liquid ambers blaze and moult in
countrified pockets,
but there is no New England fall
or quivering between freezing and meting
in cruel Aprils,
and no sense of history
here and now
in Australia.

Yet time is reflected in the season's change.

The senses do not dim,
the pleasures simpler,
the sunlight softer –
January days and weeks with nothing
on the feet but sun have
come this way before and passed –

winter's approach is not cruel,
but threadbare
like downtown Goulburn in sleet.

You left the elemental river-silt loam
for air and fire minus the ice,
and face the coming of winter
on a historyless autumn morning alone.

Sense and notion are suspended
and another shape drones in –
planes in the air suspended
mark the place where wanderlust ended –
back from England alone, in love and broke.

27. Chasing Roos at Coona

Brought there to be blooded
they were majestically long and lean
(limbs of industrial strength
steam pistons pumping
devouring distance in unheard-of times)
they had long slender faces
lit by eyes swivelling alive
tongues alive to the scent of roos

who bounded ahead
in timeless strides
jagging impossible wonderful lines

afterwards
paws splayed
in near-sphinx-like poses
they are sated from severed roo legs
only one – ours –
will never make the race tracks
his roo-ripped guts
frying to black in the quivering sun.

28. Southern Highlands Train

Some sleep gently in the same seats each trip,
having boarded the train in Goulburn,
mouths slightly open, lips fluting gently with
each exhalation –
some are in their laptop worlds,
some need to talk or be heard –
others are plugged in,
neatly severed, tiny mouse music just
audible inside their heads.
The readers are away somewhere else,
in love with a Welsh prince of the middle ages
or another planet,
but far away
from the imponderable present,
which has boredom and pain in it
and loneliness.

Time passes,
people get off
and go to jobs that must be attended,
must have attention paid to them
if dreams are to be.
The train moves,
makes animal noises
grunts shunts hisses –

there is a river crossing,
the sudden beginning of new housing estates
that spawn like lobsters
and a school by one station.

The afternoon returns us
to the familiar amphitheatre of hills,
still cattle preoccupied with grass
and wires extending to distance
like giant skeletal life savers,
feeding with raised curved arms
life lines to the drowning.

29. A River

A small boat bobs far out in a wide river
and two small figures are fishing –
the light is dazzling, the water dancing.

The ping of civilization's earliest ideas echoed through the rivers,
through the Nile valley,
the crescent-shaped Sumer,
along the Rhine, Volga, Amazon, Loire, Mississippi –
all have dark and beautiful stories well told.

But here our history is less defined by time
and the laying down of the law's silt –
our rivers twist and meander through tales
of English would-be heroes, explorers bogged down
by marshes, distance or heat or all three,
of Anglo-Irish dreams of farms and land of their own,
of yearning, calling, the ghostly leaving of tribes
harried and hunted from their shores.

Yet here a river courses like blood,
lives and pulses as undefined and unremarked as
any of its complexity and depth,
and deserves more –
it's claim is sensual not objective,
not recorded or ruled or mapped
nor traded on or gambled on,
nor fought across or crossed
by raiders seeking glory and gold –
its life is in its eddies, swirling around
a sand bar at first light,
in its many secrete places,
hidden overhangs, the sudden jump of perch,
in its smell, its moods, its memories,
its timeless motion to the sea.

I remember many years ago –
two boys in a boat fishing for their first catch,
my sons on the wide Shoalhaven,
miles from anywhere.

30. The Imperial

Every town has its own Imperial,
the name a throwback to days of
paling fences and
crackers on Empire days,
of ice-chests and
the hidden underbelly of
six o'clock closing
and things that no-one talked about –
every town, and perhaps a Railway, a Royal
or all three, perhaps a Town and Country
or a Woolpack, a Bridge, a Commercial,
Arms, a Duke of something, a Grand
and throwbacks to other times when
the Murphys, o'Malleys and Kellys were
despised and banned and drank at their own
Shamrocks, Sweeneys and Bridie O'Sheas.

Our social history is in our pubs,
a male's history shot through with
mateship and brawls,
with commercial travellers and barmaids,
with mixed lounges and
sedate shandies in ladies' waists,
convenient meetings of unions and clubs,
to miners and shearers on sprees
belting out tunes with pianos and fiddles
and thuds of boots on wood,
to the sadness of dark back door dealings for
cheap plonk to be drunk at billabongs,
and of men reduced to flogging their skills
having pissed their tomorrows away
and sicked up their innards
and subsiding into liver-blasted greyness ...
ah Henry what a sand end –
we need you as we ever did
to sing of our humanity
and give us back our souls.

Macca sits in his normal corner
having given up smoking for the tenth time and
notes that Bede has a horse he knows racing
at Gosford and should win –
"like taking wheat off a blind chook" …
later with all the regulars in
the smokers' bar is "rambunctiously" loud
and the time passes quickly
and the beer goes sweetly down.

There is an Imperial
in every town.

31. A Cell

Underneath, far underneath
the non-slip floor of the bright, stainless-cold kitchen
is a cell,
small, musty-dark and mute.
On its walls are metal brackets for chains –
all else has rotted.

It's been buried there since colonial days
and forgotten,
as a tomb in the west-bank desert.

Stick-thin, crusty-souled outcasts
were thrown in there,
outcasts
who refused to tug their locks
or kill sheep,
men not of that name but
of that breed.

The would-be gentry granted this place
surveyed the realm from shaded verandahs,
motivated of course by altruism,
not greed,
men who would of course
build a nation –
which is why they threw those souls
in the cell.

The gentry now are gone to sanctified ground
and their realm has shrunk
to golf course size,
and the cell below the clubhouse
has become a kind of dark soul place –
the local ghost tour goes there,
hoping to sniff the past
and have their eyeballs
bewildered by orbs of light.

32. Milkman and The Maggies

(for Jimmy my milkman)

The milkman was a West's selector who pinched my sister's toast
before she was able to wake up and get it,
who arrived on Christmas Day with three-quarters of
a bottle of whiskey in him, stupid bugger,
but a selector he was, so each Saturday though he
was always late he'd pick me up near Burwood pub
and we'd go to the game.

A player called Bede was often in the car,
the team hooker who swore and claimed
the selectors ignored his good games but
I actually knew he was pushed over the tryline
by a big front rower called Nev Boxhead.

I'd watch the games, yell myself hoarse
and wait with Mrs Henry outside the sheds,
listening to her complaints that her husband was
too fragile, too much a gentleman to play this silly game
but he was the only one I ever saw who
could take Yappy's passes one-handed, clasped
to his ribs which must have been like asbestos.
And there was another Darcy, a full back from
Wollongong who kicked eleven goals in his first game
and drenched President Keato with a hose in
the primitive Henson Park rooms.

Through Jimmy I got insights into the great –
the big centre's pigeons and his hatred of rock choppers,
particularly Moir who damned near froze to
death on the wing because Harry wouldn't pass,
and Yappy who never stopped and as everyone knew
was the only player in the team with any class –
he carved his way through Parra with us
down 15 – 16 and a minute left and scored

twice against the Berries in the second half
with us down 6 – 8 at the break ...

I heard Darcy's wife died of cancer.
The centre became a cranky butcher at Port,
and Yappy reffed.
And I've seen the fullback since,
playing golf, but old.

And Jimmy, my milkman,
he sold the run,
and took to training trotters at Menangle,
but his second heart attack
stopped him in his tracks last year.

And the Maggies, well they're decades past,
pre-fast-food, pre-Packer and pre-Murdoch.
And who has milkmen anymore
that deliver the stuff to the door,
and fill lonely child-hours as mine were
with memories like these?

33. A Little Spanish

Never knew much Spanish
but the idea quickly took root –
'vamonos muchacos' and 'via con dios',
meaningless kerfuffle
but part of the eye-opening
that went with first-year uni –
you know, a radical awareness,
an awakening that came
with the compunction to 'do' something
instead of just talking –
the little country,
la patria chica,
the concept of smallness, democracy Athenian-style –
no not communism Karl Marx yes yes yes
a spectre is haunting Europe and all that
but this was different this was,
well,
a concept that made sense,
smaller communities ruled over – no –
presided over by people of principle
men and women who loved freedom,
smaller communities, community leaders
elected for limited terms,
limited taxes , compassion for those
downtrodden by events they could not control,
taxes from those who had control of...

by god no wonder those political scientists were popular,
good thing to have done pol science
instead of major in English –
played squash with Ian too, associate prof
though getting into Lainey's pants
was really his go –
I told her as much
when we stopped for a roadie.
It didn't seem to worry her though –
flirtatious bitchy lovely Lainey.

We made a good threesome
Lainey, Glory-Anne and me.
We wrote some wonderfully turgid poems à la T.S.Eliot
all fire and ice, ate lentils and rice
such beautiful rhymes.

Was uni that patria chica?
Vietnam continued
and protests shouted out in chorus time,
faces flushed with righteous zeal were raucous
till the coppers came
but scaled to deafening after that,
but still we smiled our secret smiles
and arm in arm sang out our creed –
but the horses spooked
and jammed us in
and David Jones' great window snapped
and shards of glass glinted so bright
amid a red pastiche of surrealistic art.

My vacation bus driver was only my age
but what a hoot,
stopped in traffic half way up William Street
and gave the startled occupants
a swear-filled spray.
When I asked him later he said
some fucking bastard kept ringing the bells.
He got me through those broken-shift days
with bennies and dexies –
it felt so good I found a doctor
who said he could prescribe them
so long as I dealt only with him.

So in year two,
I waited at balls and cleaned after,
showered, ate and attended lectures
and accumulated distinctions
and good stories to tell –
finding a couple in post-ball coitus,
still so drunk they wanted me
as meat in their sandwich,

and tutor Mrs. P. whose sherry-fed ardour
influenced me to consider
the raunchier tales of Chaucer.

Into third year,
Gwen, a mature ager from the Shire
disappeared, reason unknown,
Lainey and Glory-Anne drifted on by,
and drunk on a cocktail of my own design
I planned my leather-elbowed future.

Jaw-gritting months, speed free,
sank me.

Rushing to the front to watch
the stripper at the Bacchus ball,
I dragged my open-mouthed girl,
toga open, laughter erupting,
nipples already the colour of blood.

And la patria chica, my own little country?
It receded to myth as myth I had made it.
The reality was a linguistic and cultural,
economic, military, liberally constituted nation,
not a universal barrio
with universal education,
more a fundamental paradox
in discourse and practice.

It was of course a long time ago.
I 'm now well past my sixtieth year
and my friend Michael,
painting my pagoda while I sit disabled by
says you long-haired uni layabouts
you protesting fucking wankers
were doing fuck-all
while I was fighting VC and
my mate got his balls shot off...
he laughs.

No comment in reply.

34. Annibal the Dental Mechanic

Like the ghost of a ball I once caught,
diving full length on Gilgandra turf in a cricket final
(I still have the ball),
Annibal has floated up from my past.
Great name that, redolent of the heroism that challenged the world
and almost won.

Back a bit, that cricket image again –
in the country town where I "trained" to teach,
I ran hard at a catch and
woke up in hospital, "mine" still ringing in my ears.
Did I yell? Did we both?
Why was his elbow longer than mine?
The mirror the nurse held threw back such an image
that even now I slowly close my eyes …
a chunked-up, pink nose,
and teeth, oh my teeth, obscenely awry.

Manray's melting clocks become the image of my mouth.

I smiled only a little after that.
The anaesthetic took away the immediate pain.
The long term pain of four front teeth,
gone missing in action, is with me still.

Annibal showed me teeth that were real,
discoloured somewhat, not glistening white,
and, quite remarkably, somewhat askew,
a little bent inward.
I somehow knew
I'd go back there again.

And I did.
I forget which South American state
he'd smuggled his family from,
but a dentist there, here he was a "dental mechanic".

His father and brother had disappeared
he casually noted.
The club he invited me to throbbed to a rhythm I didn't know
and there was a picture of Che on one wall,
and characters with bandanas smoked cigars.
I was lost but loved it,
out of my depth but laughing like I had front teeth.

I lost him at uni, in my first year.
He intended to protest on Vietnam
but when I went to his rooms his plaque was gone
and everything was cleared.

35. Anzac Day Speakers

Two women, green blazers, mid-seventies,
came to the school
for ANZAC day to talk to the girls.

"I met my husband when I was 15
but he went to New Guinea in 1942.
Didn't come back till 1944.
I was only 18 by then and we were married.
He died at 43."

They won the respect of children
and their spontaneous applause.

Later at the staff morning tea:
It was very hard.
He died of cancer.
War related?
Oh no they said no.
My daughter was only six
but I was working at the time.
At first it was terrible.
I gave my neighbour a key.
Malaria – you know what it does?
He was back in the war and
had his hands around my throat
the kids were screaming ...
Did I say I had four?
A condition related to the war?
Oh they said it'll go away.
It didn't.
No we paid our own bills.
Twelve hundred dollars the operation cost.
The youngest got some help through legacy
but that's not Veterans Affairs you see.
Oh some war widows got pensions we know.
Each time I've fought for some and won
I've felt real good

but I can't get it for myself ...
but I'm seventy-five
and each day I'm alive now
I just take it as it comes.
Got married two months back
didn't I Kath?
Poor Kath – her husband was British,
in Burma you see, in the army at fourteen
but they burnt all the records
so she can't prove a thing.
Died several years ago.
Kath and I and several others
go on long trips. Nominated driver me.
If we're going for one day, we'll stay over
and stay for three.
I'm too tired to fight any more.
At Veterans Affairs
I sat at a table under a lamp,
they were at tables without any lights,
I said "You too ashamed to show your
bloody faces?
What'd youse do in the war?"
I think they stamped my papers then.
Couldn't be bothered fighting any more.
Legal? Oh yes we had legal people
but I like to talk for myself I do –
what would the legal people know about me?
It was very very hard but it's over now,
it's over for me and Kath,
isn't it love?"

36. Formal

The last image we saw of the students
obliterated the first, of tuxedos and lace –
leftovers,
sitting, squatting, lying at the gate,
near comatose and besotted.

They were there in natural arrogance when we arrived –
"Shore" said a young brave swiftly sipping champagne in
excitement and anticipation, maybe fear, and
inner suburban socialites bobbed everywhere –
taxis and Mercs flowed to the entrance
as we moved upstairs through the old stone monastery –
at one stage in the evening
the toilet floors were slippery with vomit.

When we left, the last of them were at the gate –
the feast was finished, tuxedos were gone,
shirt tails flapping and
a wine stained dress with red against white
was the image of lost innocence,
was the blood of wedding sheets without the ceremony.

37. Michael's Garlic Crop

Michael sits on board head up and happy
like a helmsman,
with the tractor dipping and rolling
across the paddock sea.
It will be well drained,
both sides sloping gently
towards the creek,
a swell of landscape
which will grow garlic.

He is a former psychiatric nurse
who changes car engines to suit
car bodies, always Peugeots
because he loves these cars
with a tenderness
that somehow was missing with women.
His teenage daughter now prefers
her friends on the North Coast
and has missed these holidays.
He has two bedrooms and
a living room, no hot water,
an outside loo at the back of the house
and way down the hill,
the village of Bendemeer
and its pub.
His relatives live across the paddock
and he is glad of that
for his sister-in-law, he says,
is killing
the relationship with his brother.

We hitch a log
to the thingos at the back of the tractor
so the turkey shit can be spread
and after a while,
the fine dust doesn't
smell that bad as it settles on my face.

The garlic seeds are coming,
50 kilos of Italian White,
50 more of this and that.
It's infectious –
a local cattle worker
has offered Michael an acre
of his own on the river flat.

At the pub last night,
we agree that our kids seemed well,
having come through
the fracturing,
the tendon-tearing-and-ripping splits,
the break-ups,
near insanity, drunkenness.

As the tractor wheels
and works back up the slope,
he is smiling.
It will be his first garlic crop.

38. The Ruined Lighthouse at Cape St George

It was built because ships were foundering along the coast.
After the original site was moved
the tendering and building were clouded by
lack of appropriate consultation –
it was called Cape St George,
no doubt after that dragon-slaying saint
the spirit of England,
Shakespeare's hero at Harfleur and Agincourt.

Far distant but visible,
across the swell is
the steepling perpendicular named by Cook,
and down a way Aboriginal Wreck Bay
whose white identity was forged
by loss of life on British ships.

But the lighthouse didn't last –
a father drowned fishing for sharks,
a daughter had her head blown off,
one body not found
the other interred in lonely ground.
The residence and the lighthouse were blown up
and there it is noted on the site plaque
the problem ended.

Now limestone blocks lie strewn askew
guarded by bars,
and a viewing platform juts out
where once the cliff gave way to
one who fell below,
somewhere in the bone-white sand.

39. Overtaken

He gave us the finger
tongue flicking and poking
like a small dog's penis
his eyes popping
in near orgasmic glee
mini trampolining in his seat
and the car he was in
pulled past us in
a blather and swirl
careening wildly
cascading us with
a brilliant shower
of brown-yellow dust,
a million particles of the desert.

As fast as that,
the sun came through again.

In the autumn late-day light,
in a colour not modern,
the dwindling cloud that was a car
was swallowed by the old dust,
was swallowed by time.